# Instant Charisma

*A Quick and Easy Guide To Talk, Impress And Make Anyone Like You*

By Michele Gilbert

<u>Visit My Amazon Author Page</u>

I0478698

Dedicated to those who choose to stretch beyond their own limits and to seek a more abundant and fulfilling life.

Your thoughts are creative.

Michele Gilbert

# My Free Gift To You!

As a way of saying thank you for downloading my book, I am willing to give you access to a selected group of readers who (every week or so) receive inspiring, life-changing kindle books at deep discounts, and sometimes even absolutely free.

Wouldn't it be great to get amazing Kindle offers delivered directly to your inbox?

Wouldn't it be great to be the first to know when I'm releasing new fresh and above all sharply discounted content?

## But why would I do something like this?

Why would I offer my books at such a low price and even give them away for free when they took me countless hours to produce?

**Simple…. Because I Want To Spread The Word.!**

For a few short days Amazon allows Kindle authors to promote their newly released books by offering them deeply discounted (up to 70% price discounts and even for free. This allows us to spread the word extremely quickly allowing users to download thousands and thousands of copies in a very short period of time.

Once the timeframe has passed, these books will revert back to their normal selling price. That's why you will benefit from being the first to know when they can be downloaded for free!

**So are you ready to claim your weekly Kindle books?**

You are just one click away! Follow the link below and sign up to start receiving awesome content

Thank you and Enjoy!

# Table of contents

# Introduction

I want to thank you and congratulate you for downloading this book. You have made your first step towards becoming the kind of person you have always wanted to be. And what kind of person is that? Well, the type of person who can meet new people, break the ice, make connections, and instantly leave an impression in any situation. This may seem like a tall order, but by using time-tested strategies and perspectives from some of the most influential and respected individuals, in no time you will be striking up conversations and using your new-found charisma to enhance your interactions and get the most out of socializing.

Presented in this book are strategies for initiating conversations and letting everyone you meet know that you are a stunning conversationalist. You will learn how to engage people in any situation. You will learn how to make a conversation a pleasant experience for everyone. You will learn some common mistakes to avoid. And finally, you will learn some foolproof strategies for connecting with individuals and leaving a lasting impression.

So, if you are ready to take charge of your interactions and begin making lasting impressions on everyone you meet, then let's get you started on a path to instant charisma.

Thanks again for downloading this book, I hope you enjoy it!

# CHAPTER 1
## The Art of Engagement

Survey after survey has confirmed that public speaking is more feared than death. Some individuals may even experience physical maladies in apprehension of speaking publically. However, for some, speaking to a new acquaintance can be just as frightening. And, even if one lacks the apprehension that some may feel when speaking to someone for the first time, they may find their conversation skills are lacking and insufficient for their social needs. They may find themselves walking away from an encounter embarrassed and unsure of how the other person feels about them. These feelings can be very disheartening and can even lead one to avoid new encounters. Furthermore, conversational ineptitude can have many negative consequences.

What people think of us based on our interactions is extremely important to us in a variety of ways. In a professional sense, we benefit greatly by being a part of an information network. We discover useful information about opportunities, openings, ways to enrich our skillset, and countless other things. In our personal lives we also benefit by being in a well-connected network. Some of the same benefits we get from being well connected professional remain true for our personal lives. By having a healthy personal network we open ourselves up to rewarding and fulfilling relationships that can change our lives for the better. However, developing and maintaining a healthy personal and professional network hinges on your ability to engage in effective conversation.

As humans, our ability to interact and communicate with other humans is critical. This has been the case since the dawn of time and remains to be true today. Put simply, communication is necessary for our survival. While our methods of survival have drastically changed since the Stone Age, our need for communication has remained. Nevertheless, in our current environment of instant global communication, our face-to-face communication skills are taking a back seat to our electronic communication skills. However, face-to-face communication will never lose its importance.

Just like any skill, communication can be improved by learning new techniques or strategies, and by putting this newly learned information to work by incorporating it into our daily lives. The very first thing you must understand when it comes to conversation is how to engage with people. Engaging with people you have never met, or even with those you have known for many years, requires you to be proactive. Often, you must be the first to initiate the interaction. Having to be the initiator may be a source of anxiety for some. But, if you keep an open mind and keep focused on your personal reasons for wanting to improve your communication skills, then all that is left is to absorb the strategies presented in this book. After that, you will possess everything you need to increase your charisma and be an effective communicator in any situation.

### The Perceptive Approach

The key to engaging with anyone at any time is being able to read a situation. Much like you read a book or advertisement, your brain is constantly "reading" everything around you at all times. Much of this, however, is going on behind the scenes. Millions of years of evolution have made our brains quite effective at taking in and processing information at lightening quick speeds. But, there are many things our brains read that we are aware of. When we look at someone for the first time, our brain makes a series of judgments. Is this person a threat? Are they a suitable mate? This is totally out of our control. However, we make a lot of judgments based on our knowledge, experiences, or how we have been socialized.

You should put both of these processes (i.e. your conscious judgments and subconscious judgments) to work as you approach someone. What can you tell about someone by just looking at them? Well, if you develop this skill, then you will be able to garner a lot of information about someone before you even shake their hand. Some people are naturally perceptive, inclined to be able to discern how someone is feeling or even their personality traits by simply looking at them. However, don't fear if you are not naturally perceptive. You can get better by practicing.

Go to any public space, like a bar, restaurant, park, or even a library. Pick a spot and sit down with a book or magazine. Take time and examine (covertly, of course) those around you. Try to deduce as much as you can about them. What does what they are wearing or how they carry themselves say about their personality? Do they look tired or overworked? Are they confident, shy, angry, or indifferent? How do they interact with others? Avoid coming to extreme conclusions or making firm judgments when the information is incomplete. And even though being able to discern information through observation is a valuable skill, making rash judgments can have adverse effects and lead to embarrassment and misunderstanding, exactly what you are trying to avoid.

Once you have sharpened your perceptive eye, put your skills to use. When you approach someone, you will now have an advantage you didn't have before- the advantage of knowledge. When you enter in to a conversation with a better idea of how your conversation partner is feeling or thinking the benefits will be instant and twofold. Firstly, you will have a more informed view of how you should interact with your conversation target. It doesn't make much sense to interact the same way with someone who is jovial and with someone who is tired and in a bad mood. Secondly, by catering your conversation to the feelings and personality to your conversation target you will be communicating an interest in them in a positive, organic, and genuine manner. There is nothing more distasteful than someone who creates false interest for the sake of conversation. It may be effective in the short term, but many will detect your lack of sincerity and their impression of you will not be a good one.

### Body Language

Besides your perceptive abilities, engaging with someone is greatly aided by an awareness and use of body language. Everyone knows that body language makes up the majority of our communication. This is almost cliché in any conversation it appears. However, the truth of the statement is undeniable. As mentioned above, our brain makes a series of quick judgments whenever we encounter someone. Our brain does all this based on what it reads. And what it reads is primarily the body language of the individual. How they stand, the orientation of their facial muscles (or from another point of view, their emotions), and their eye movements are all processed instantaneously so that we can make a judgment on what to do.

Conversely, the target of conversation is doing the exact same thing as you approach. Everything from your posture to your smile makes an instant impression with someone. Put this scientific reality to work for you and use your body language to your benefit. Entire volumes could be written on the subject of body language and how to use it to reach desired effects. However, starting out, the best thing you can do is simply to be aware of your own body language. By being conscious of your own body language, you will likely express your emotions and intentions much more clearly through your body.

Also, besides simply having an awareness of your body language, you can take practical steps to conveying positive body language. As mentioned above, posture is incredibly important, but why? Well someone who exhibits a strong, erect posture exudes confidence and self-assurance. Furthermore, a good posture enables your voice to have more strength. While vocal strength is a quality normally desired for more formal public speaking situations, strength of voice also carries with it control over one's voice. This, of course, is very important when speaking to someone for the first time. Other than a strong posture, a genuine and full smile is another practical strategy you can employ to engage with others.

As our brains read other individual's faces, we are apt to mimic their facial expressions. There are specific cells in human brains that facilitate these reactions. These cells are called mirror neurons. They are the reason smiles can seem to be contagious, or that an angry scowl can put a damper on your mood. It has even been suggested that sociopaths and other individuals who lack the ability to emphasize and relate to other individuals may have something wrong with their mirror neurons. Put simply, when you smile it puts the person to whom you are smiling at greater ease. But if you feel that your smile is lacking, then simply practice. You are well aware of how a genuine smile feels on your face. Try to mimic those movements with your facial muscles in front of a mirror. After all, every muscle in our body can be trained and improved. So, why not your facial muscles, as well? However, all the positive body language in the world can't help you if you don't know what to say after saying "hello" for the first time. Next, let's try and understand the principles of what makes a good conversation.

# CHAPTER 2
# Making Conversation Enjoyable

There is almost nothing worse than being in a social situation where you have no clue what to say, the conversation dwindles to silence, and then you part ways feeling embarrassed and hoping you don't run into them again. Fortunately, an unpleasant situation such as this can be avoided by understanding what makes a good conversation and how to make a conversation worthwhile for both you and your conversation partner. If you consider your social skills to be lacking, this may seem like a daunting task. But just like every big problem, breaking the problem into smaller and more approachable problems is a great strategy for overcoming.

## *A Good Conversation is Hard to Find*

What makes a good conversation? Firstly, what is a conversation? It is a word that everyone knows the meaning of, yet fails to consider the implications of its meaning. When you converse with someone you are engaging in an act of communication. Communication, in turn, is a process of sending and receiving information, implying the involvement of more than one individual or entity. When fireflies make their early-evening displays, they are communicating. Their communication, however, isn't as complex as a discussion about politics or theoretical physics. Nevertheless, it meets the qualifications of communication. The point here is that communication is evident all around us. Communication is natural. So, then why does is seem to be so difficult for us humans to communicate sometimes?

There are several factors that make communication between humans difficult at times. Firstly, language is a complex mechanism. Some individuals have better command of the language in which they speak. Some know the precise words to convey what they are attempting to express at any turn of the conversation. Others, however, do not. Secondly, socialization is a key element to understand how we interact with each other. Some individuals grow and develop in a more social atmosphere, prompting them to develop social interaction skills faster, while others are less socially developed. Thirdly, our ability to communicate hinges on our ability to receive and process information quickly. Sometimes we forget that the brain is a physical organ. Its process is all physical in nature. So are our thoughts and speech. This means that we can suffer from physical limitations when it comes to communication. This could be as severe as a neurological disorder, but also could be as minor as your brain not being as effective at communication when experiencing a stressful social situation. These are some general reasons why conversation can prove difficult, but most of these problems can be easily addressed. And, keep in mind that just because you don't have any of the abovementioned issues, that doesn't mean that your conversation partner doesn't.

### Conversation Made Easy

So, having now understood some basic principles of conversation and the reasons it can sometimes be difficult, you will now learn some excellent strategies for improving the quality of your conversations. Firstly, a good conversation doesn't start when you meet someone, but well before. The best conversationalists are those who have something to say. If you find that when you converse with new people or past acquaintances and you feel like you never have anything to say, then you need to gather material for conversation. The best way to do this is to continue to educate yourself. Stay up-to-date with the news, go see a new movie, listen to a new album, or go see a new art exhibit. People instinctively are interested in new things. If you are well familiar with what is up and coming and recent you will be interesting because people with have a tangible aspect to associate you with.

But what if who you are talking to isn't interested in the new movie or album? Well, outside of traveling time or seeing into the future, it is impossible to know what another individual is passionate about *before* you get to know them through conversation. However, you know exactly what *you* are passionate about. If you pursue you passions honestly and intently you will always be interesting. People enjoy talking to someone who is passionate. This piece advice comes with a small caveat, however. It is okay to be passionate about your interests and be comfortable talking about those things to others. But, avoid talking about your passions that may be controversial in a first-time meeting. Also, don't talk about your passions solely. The reason you should pursue your passions is that those who are active participants in their own lives are intrinsically more interesting. But, don't forget that other individuals have their own passions and interests. Think of a new conversation as a way to express your interests to a new person and learn about theirs, as well.

Besides staying current and pursuing your passions, there are a few other things you can do to ensure your conversation will be pleasant and enjoyable. Most people think of a conversation as a back-and-forth process, but in action, they treat it more as a staged performance, where they are an actor on stage and the person with whom they are speaking is the audience. Avoid this type of mentality. If you approach conversation as a laundry list of things you need to say before the conversation ends, then whomever you are speaking to will feel as if they are being *spoken to*. Instead, make sure the conversation is inclusive by making the goal of conversation to be about mutual understanding and learning, rather than a free, unsolicited informational session about yourself.

Furthermore, treat the conversation as a living thing. If you didn't follow the advice in the last paragraph, then your conversation will likely have the feel of an infomercial sales pitch. Avoid this by treating the conversation as a dynamic entity, one that is subject to change. In short, give your conversation some breathing room by letting it flow. To let your conversation flow, don't be set on controlling every aspect of it. Don't go at it with certain ends in mind other than to get to know someone and let them get to know you. If you are intentionally directing the conversation, it may have an off-putting effect. This could lead to your conversation partner not wanting to open up and participate in the conversation. If you find this part of your conversation skills lacking, then try to listen and take clues from your conversation partner. Another great method for keeping a conversation natural and flowing is to ask questions. Ask your conversation partner quests from time to time. By putting the ball in their court, you share the control over the conversation and also keep it from becoming stale

There are countless things you could do to improve your conversational skills. Utilizing these basic strategies is a good first step towards becoming a better conversationalist. However, the greatest and most effective thing you can do is to practice. With practice, you will become more skilled at paying attention to the cues your conversation partner gives you. The only thing that really separates the poor or mediocre conversationalist from the great conversationalist is the commitment to getting better and amount of practice invested.

# CHAPTER 3
## What You Shouldn't Do

Sometimes is it easier to express what someone *shouldn't* do. This is especially true for conversation. In fact, the list of *don'ts* is certainly much longer than any list of *dos*. The reason for this is quite simple. While there are some hard rules in conversation, everyone is an individual with a unique personality. One strategy may work for one individual with a certain personality, while another individual using the same strategy may falter. However, there are some things to avoid no matter who you are and no matter your personality type. Avoiding these 5 common mistakes will ensure that your conversation is enjoyable and, more importantly, memorable for good reasons.

### Don't be oblivious of the situation

Being aware of you place and setting is essential in any conversation. Striking up a conversation at a library or in a workplace is completely different than striking up a conversation at a bar or a sporting event. Although, this advice may seem obvious, transgressions against situational decorum can have very bad effects. For one, it will show your conversation partner that you are oblivious to social cues. And, that is not the sort of message you want to convey right off the bat. Another aspect to this common mistake is to not contradict the dynamics of all the individuals present. If the target of your conversation is with a group, then don't neglect the group for sake of the individual. Instead, use the situation to your advantage. A discussion at a library can easily shift to interests in literature or really any topic. A discussion at a sporting event or bar with live music can equally be used to your advantage to begin the conversation with at least some common ground. A discussion within a group, rather than in a one-on-on situation can remove a lot of pressure.

### Don't try too hard

Above, you learned to try to make your conversation flow by making it a mutual effort. Similarly, don't make the mistake of trying too hard. You don't want your conversation to seem forced. This makes a conversation seem wooden and uninteresting. It is natural to feel as if you should be saying something, yet not feel words naturally flowing from you. In this situation, focus on listening. While your conversation partner speaks, don't think of what you are going to say next, but listen intently. By providing your attention you will free yourself from overacting or focusing too hard on figuring out what to say.

### Don't use aggressive body language

Earlier, you learned about the use of body language. Don't forget that body language is used when we threated and intimidate others. Try to use welcoming and non-confrontational body language. Avoid excess eye-contact. Also, make sure you respect the physical boundaries of those with whom you speak. By using your smile, a reasonable physical distance, and open and friendly gestures you will present an air of trustworthiness and pleasantness. Remember, these types of qualities will ensure your conversation goes well.

### Don't be afraid of silence

A good conversation is all about balance. While excess silence in a conversation can seem awkward and be undesirable, the lack of silence can have the same effect. Furthermore, if you are speaking yourself to breathlessness, you are likely speaking too much. Don't be afraid to pause every now and then. Pauses in conversation are perfectly natural and often serve to emphasize our speech.

### Don't talk too much

Lastly, avoid talking too much. Give your conversation partner ample chances to speak. The last thing you want is a one-sided conversation. Also, you can't talk and listen at the same time. Focus on doing one at a time and you will be well on your way to becoming a great conversationalist.

# CHAPTER 4
## Leaving an Impression

If you have absorbed everything in this ebook so far, then you will already have a good idea of what makes a good conversation. You will also understand the sorts of things that will ensure the quality of your conversation is above average. Furthermore, you are aware of the most common mistakes that people make when engaging in conversation with new and old acquaintances alike. Now, the last thing you must learn is how to leave a good impression. If you follow all of the advice in this ebook so far, you are already halfway there to understanding the principles of making a good impression.

The first step to making a good impression is having a good first encounter. After all, you only are allowed one first impression with a new person. Make it count by following all the principles outlined in this ebook. Sometimes things do not go as well as planned, however. Just remember impressions cannot be replaced, but they certainly can be improved upon. If the first encounter did not go as well as you desired, then try and understand what went wrong and give it another go. Try and make light of the situation and continue to be easygoing. This will show strength of character

The next step is to be conscious of not only your needs, but also the needs of your conversation partner. This could be as simple as giving attention to what they have to say while they are speaking. Or, it could be as important as give them vital information, like a job opening or other types of information they may find beneficial or valuable. In fact, if you enter into a conversation with a "winner takes all" mindset, and you intend to win the conversation, then your conversation partner will likely have little interest in continuing to speak with you. Instead, approach conversations with a "win-win" attitude. Focus on how each of you gain benefit from the interaction. This simple shift in mindset can have amazing results, making your conversation partner comfortable and sure of your mutually beneficial intentions.

Lastly, don't put all your focus on the actual words you are using. While what you say is important. It is unlikely that whomever you are speaking to will remember precisely what you said to them. They will likely only remember the highlights of what you said. If they have an exceptional memory, then they may remember a few phrases. Nevertheless, it is extremely unlikely that anyone you will speak to will remember everything you said when they speak to you. However, they will remember how you made them feel. This is a very useful piece of conventional wisdom. Focus on making your conversational partner feel at ease, appreciated, and understood. This is by far the greatest thing you can do to ensure that you make a lasting impression.

# Conclusion

I hope this book was able to help you understand the principles of conversation that may have eluded your interactions until now. Utilize these skills for the benefit of yourself and those around you. Don't be surprised by the benefits awarded to the charismatic!

The next step is to put these principles, strategies, and ways of thinking to work for you today. Remember, everything presented in this book can be acquired through simple understanding and diligent practice.

Thank you again for downloading this book!

I hope it was able to help you to feel more comfortable around people and be able to let your true self shine through with winning and impressive conversations.

The next step is to take action and not procrastinate!

Before you go, I'd like to say thank you for purchasing my book.

I know you could have picked so many other books to read getting over negativity and living a more positive life. So A Big thanks for downloading this book and reading it all the way to completion.

Now I would like to ask a small favor.

Could you please click here to leave a review for this book on Amazon?

The feedback will help me continue to publish more kindle books that will help people to get better results in their lives.

And if you found it helpful in anyway then please let me know :-)

Thank you and good luck!

# Preview of My New Book

Body Language 101

What A Person's Body Language Is Really Telling You... And How You Can Use It To Your Advantage

## Talk to the Hand

I don't know about you, but when I watch shows like *Lie to Me* or *Sherlock*, so often, I really, really wish that I could be that good. Heck, after I watched *The Mentalist* for the first time, I was studying everyone. I stared at footprints trying to see if I could tell whether the person walking was right handed or left handed. Not only is this super impractical for me as an actual skill, but it's super addicting. The thing is, it's all about studying people and watching them, but there's a science to it. I may not be out there catching criminals red handed for having a nervous tell, but it has helped me read situations and understand things that I previously missed.

So sure, you might not catch your arch-nemesis, but you might be able to understand things a little better with a little study of body language. And that's why I'm here. Body language is not just for detectives out there looking to catch murderers and thieves. Body language is the key to understanding the unspoken words that our body is communicating so heavily without our knowledge. Not only will this help you understand and relate to people better, but it'll make it so that you are aware of your own presence to others.

Nonverbal communication makes up the majority of our communication and most of us are clueless to the actual comprehension and understanding of it. That means that those who do not invest time in learning what to say in our nonverbal appearance are missing so much. But the truth is, we don't miss all of it. We have come to silently absorb and understand nonverbal communication, regardless of whether we know it or not. It's the art of learning to understand something we already know and to heighten our understanding and acceptance of what's being communicated to us. It's tricky, I know, but it's not impossible to understand.

What I'm going to tell you in this book is going to make sense to you and a lot of it is going to feel familiar, like you already knew that. Well, the reason for that is that you you've been picking up these silent transmissions for years, you just haven't acknowledged them or put a name to some of the habits you've already taught yourself.

So stick around and start to see if you can't agree or relate to some of the information you're going to receive. But more importantly, I want to address your homework before we start getting into the gritty, deep stuff. For instance, I want you to start watching people around you.

Observation is the birth of understanding and without a true sense of observance or a keen eye for noticing the little things, you're not going to pick up on some of these traits. When someone is talking to you, you're going to need to start watching them. Notice how they're standing, note the posture, have you looked at their eyes, what about the overall harmony of their face, and what are they doing with their hands? All of these things need to be running through your mind to really catch what is being conveyed to you. But not just watching their body, note the tones they're using, and the words that they're selecting. These are all going to tell you what sort of body language comes with certain attitudes and emotions. It all ties together and it is all relevant when it comes to understanding body language. So start opening your eyes and let's have a look at what they're trying to say to you.

Are you ready?

# Weapons of Mass Induction

Though Sherlock Holmes often touts his use of deductive reasoning, it is actually the opposite that we're going to focus on with you, because right now, you're a student. For those of you that do not know, inductive reasoning starts with observations that slowly build a pattern that you will then form into a hypothesis until it is proven right or wrong. If you're right, then you have a theory.

For example, Kayla touches her hair a lot when she talks to Hot Mike, but not when she's talking to anyone else. So, every time I see Kayla talking to Hot Mike and she's touching her hair, that might be a cue that she likes Hot Mike. So, until I'm proven wrong, I'm certain that I have a theory that when a woman likes a man, she'll touch her hair unconsciously.

Viola, you have just jumped from observation to theory until proven wrong. Of course, when you're Sherlock Holmes level, you'll be using the art of deductive reasoning which starts at a theory and then tested with a hypothesis and observations until you have a conclusion. I think it's time for another example to prove this one to you.

Click Here To Read The Rest of

Body Language 101

What A Person's Body Language Is Really Telling You… And How You Can Use It To Your Advantage

P.S. You'll find many more books like this and others under my name Michele Gilbert.

**Don't miss them… here is a short list.**

Wicca: The Ultimate Beginners Guide For Witches and Warlocks: Learn Wicca Magic

The Introvert's Advantage: The Introverts Guide To Succeeding In An Extrovert World

Stop Playing Mind Games: How To Free Yourself Of Controlling And Manipulating Relationships

Instant Charisma: A Quick And Easy Guide To Talk, Impress, And Make Anyone Like You

Chakras: Understanding The 7 Main Chakras For Beginners: The Ultimate Guide To Chakra Mindfulness, Balance and Healing

Practicing Mindfulness: Living in the moment through Meditation: Everyday Habits and Rituals to help you achieve inner peace

Adrenal Fatigue: What Is Adrenal Fatigue Syndrome And How To Reset Your Diet And Your Life

Sleep Tight: Overcome Insomnia and Sleep Disorders for a better more restful sleep!

Stop Back Pain Now!: Back Pain Remedies and Treatments so you can live a pain free life!

The Arthritis Pain Cure: How to find Arthritis Pain Relief and live a happy pain free life!

The Headache Pain Cure: How to find Headache Pain Relief and live a happy Pain Free Life!

Stop Panic Attacks and Anxiety Disorders without Drugs Now!: Overcome Panic, Stress and Anxiety and live a happy pain free life!

The Breakup Recovery Guide: Advice for Surviving Heartbreak, Letting Go and Thriving in an exciting new life!

The Friendship Guide to Finding Friends Forever: How to Find, Make and Keep Quality Friendships After your Breakup

How To Stop Being Jealous And Insecure: Overcome Insecurity And Relationship Jealousy

Psychic Development: Your Guide To Unlocking Your Psychic Abilities

So I Am Dating A Psychopath: Now What?

The Mind Of A Sociopath: Your Guide to Understanding The Anti-Social Personality Disorder of Sociopaths

## About Michele

Michele Gilbert was born and raised in Brooklyn, New York. Drawn to literature and writing at a young age, she enrolled at Brooklyn College and majored in English. After graduation Michele did not begin writing immediately, instead she embarked on a career in the finance industry and spent the next thirty years on Wall Street.

Serendipity struck when she least expected it. After ending a long-term relationship, Michele found herself lost and unsure what the future held. She began to read books on grief and loss, looking for answers. Those led her to delve deeper into the Law of Attraction and its power. What resulted was remarkable. Not only had she begun to heal, she had also rekindled her former love of writing and discovered her life's purpose.

The years have taken her through many twists and turns, but she learned valuable lessons along the way. Today she publishes books-mostly self-help and metaphysical in nature-and feels compelled to share her knowledge with those facing similar experiences. Her greatest hope is to inspire others and show them ways to overcome adversity and gracefully accept life's inevitable low points.

Going forward, she plans to incorporate more teachings of self-help, finance and meditation. Regular meditation is very beneficial to her progress as she forges a new life. Morning rituals and positive incantations are other practices Michele embraces; they are very restorative in daily life.

As an avid hiker, Michele and fellow club members often hike the picturesque Jersey Pine Barrens. She is a history buff, voracious reader, baseball fanatic and a foodie. She also proudly supports Trout Unlimited-a national non-profit organization dedicated to conserving, protecting and restoring North America's Coldwater fisheries and their watersheds.

Michele currently resides forty minutes from Atlantic City and the Jersey Shore. She makes her home with a Blue Russian rescue cat named Jersey, though she isn't exactly sure who rescued who.

Michele really enjoys publishing books that can make a difference in people's lives. If you have any suggestions or would like to have a specific topic covered in a future book, please send an email to michelegilbertbooks@gmail.com and we will get back to you.

Thanks for reading!

www.ingramcontent.com/pod-product-compliance
Lightning Source LLC
Chambersburg PA
CBHW041617180526
45159CB00002BC/898